THE ATTACK ON
FORT SUMTER

A DAY THAT CHANGED AMERICA

by Isaac Kerry

CAPSTONE PRESS
a capstone imprint

Published by Capstone Press, an imprint of Capstone
1710 Roe Crest Drive, North Mankato, Minnesota 56003
capstonepub.com

Library of Congress Cataloging-in-Publication Data
Names: Kerry, Isaac, author.
Title: The attack on Fort Sumter : a day that changed America / Isaac Kerry.
Other titles: Days that changed America.
Description: North Mankato : Capstone Press, [2023] | Series: Days that changed America | Includes bibliographical references and index. | Audience: Ages 8-11 | Audience: Grades 4-6 | Summary: "On April 9, 1861, soldiers gathered outside Fort Sumter. They were fighting for the Confederacy, which was made up of southern states that had left the United States. The soldiers demanded the U.S. Army leave the fort. Even though the fort had less than a week's worth of supplies, the Army refused. Three days later, a fight for the fort began. That battle was the start of the Civil War. Now readers can step back in time to learn about what led up to this historic conflict, how the costly event unfolded, and the ways in which one explosive day changed America forever"-- Provided by publisher.
Identifiers: LCCN 2021061417 (print) | LCCN 2021061418 (ebook) | ISBN 9781666341621 (hardcover) | ISBN 9781666341638 (paperback) | ISBN 9781666341645 (pdf) | ISBN 9781666341669 (kindle edition)
Subjects: LCSH: Fort Sumter (Charleston, S.C.)--Siege, 1861--Juvenile literature.
Classification: LCC E471.1 .K47 2023 (print) | LCC E471.1 (ebook) | DDC 973.7/31--dc23/eng/20211217
LC record available at https://lccn.loc.gov/2021061417
LC ebook record available at https://lccn.loc.gov/2021061418

Editorial Credits
Editor: Book Buddy Media

Consultant Credits
Richard Bell
Associate Professor of History
University of Maryland, College Park

Image Credits
Alamy: Archive Images, 5-Apr, Chicago History Museum, 22, Chronicle, 16, Stocktrek Images, Inc., 13; Getty Images: Bettmann, 9, 25, ilbusca, 6, mikroman6, 19; Library of Congress: Hirst D. Milhollen/Donald H. Mugridge, Cover, Lloyd Ostendorf, 15; Shutterstock: David Smart, 27, Everett Collection, 11, 14, 21, 24, f11photo, 7, meunierd, 23; The New York Public Library: Emmet Collection of Manuscripts Etc. Relating to American History, 12; Wikimedia: AdrienF69, 20, E. C. Kropp Co., Milwaukee, 18

Source Notes
Page 17, "A geographical line…" "Confederate States of America—Declaration of the Immediate Causes Which Induce and Justify the Secession of South Carolina from the Federal Union," Yale Law School Lillian Goldman Law Library, April 26, 1852, https://avalon.law.yale.edu/19th_century/csa_scarsec.asp, Accessed December 9, 2021

TABLE OF CONTENTS

Words in **bold** are in the glossary.

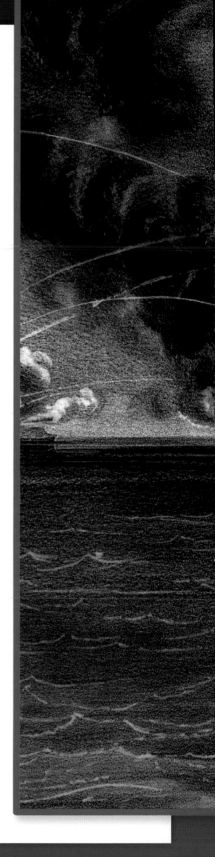

It was early morning on April 12, 1861, in Charleston, South Carolina. Suddenly, an **artillery** round flew through the sky. It exploded in a flash of light. Its target was Fort Sumter and the soldiers of the United States Army who waited inside. This was the first shot fired of the Civil War (1861–1865). But it would not be the last. Confederate troops aimed 43 cannons at the fort. Over the next two days, they would fire more than 3,300 times.

FACT

Soldiers in the North were known as Union or Federal troops. Soldiers in the South were called Confederates.

Fire destroyed the main gates and living quarters inside the fort.

CHAPTER 1

THE SLOW MARCH TO WAR

The first enslaved people arrived in America as early as the 1500s. Southern planters used slave labor to plant crops like tobacco and cotton. Growing these crops required many workers. More demand for the crops meant more workers were needed. Enslaved labor was cheap. In 1783, there were fewer than 700,000 enslaved people in the South. By 1860, there were almost 4 million.

Enslavement played a major role in the Civil War.

Most states in the North did not use enslaved people to fuel their economy. By 1804, enslavement had been outlawed in all northern states. The change took time. In some places, it took a long time. Tension over the future of slavery had been growing. Northern **abolitionists** wanted it banned everywhere in the country. They saw slavery as morally wrong. Southern plantation owners were afraid they would lose power to make their own laws.

The huge plantations of the South were built and maintained by slave labor.

FACT

Before the Civil War, there were more enslaved people than free in South Carolina and Mississippi.

As America grew, the question of equality in new states grew. In 1819, Missouri wanted to join the country. The North wanted it to be a free state. The South was afraid that more free states would mean an end to their way of life.

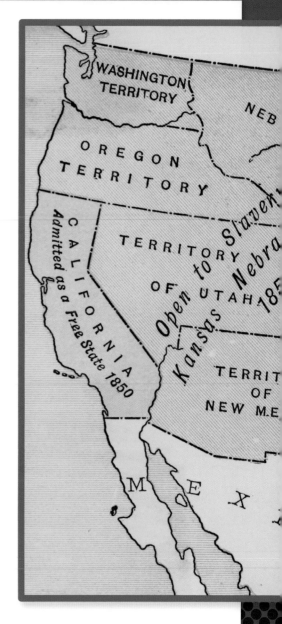

Eventually, the Missouri Compromise was created. Missouri would join the United States at the same time as Maine. Maine would be a free state. Missouri would be a slave state. This solved the issue at the time, but it didn't fix the real problem. Support for abolition continued growing in the North. A new anti-slavery **political party**, the Republican Party, formed in 1854.

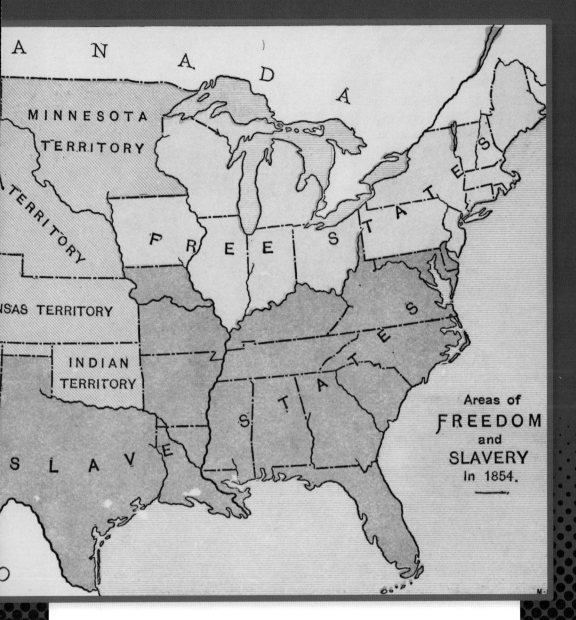

slave states and free states in 1854

CHAPTER 2

THE FORTS OF CHARLESTON HARBOR

The U.S. Army had forts all over the country. Many were on the coast and were meant to fight off enemy ships. The city of Charleston, South Carolina, had three working forts in its harbor. Fort Moultrie dated back to the Revolutionary War (1775–1783). It was located on Sullivan Island. The island stood over the harbor. Its huge cannons would have clear shots at enemy ships as they sailed past.

Castle Pinckney was a smaller fort deeper in the harbor. Its job was to finish off any ships that made it past Moultrie.

The third was Fort Sumter. It was across the harbor from Fort Moultrie. This was so any enemy ships would be caught in a **crossfire**. It could hold 650 troops. It was armed with 135 cannons. Building had begun in 1829. By 1860, it was nearly finished.

Charleston Harbor formed where the Cooper and Ashley Rivers meet. Its location was ideal for transporting goods.

During peacetime, the **garrisons** at the Charleston forts were nowhere near full strength. The entire U.S. Army had fewer than 16,000 troops. Around 85 soldiers were stationed at Fort Moultrie. Castle Pinckney and Fort Sumter had a handful of soldiers watching over them.

By 1860, Fort Moultrie had been neglected and rebuilt twice.

FACT

Major Robert Anderson was severely wounded during a battle in the Mexican-American War.

In late November 1860, Major Robert Anderson arrived in Charleston. He took command of the forces there. Major Anderson was a lifelong soldier. He had faced battle. His personal experiences left him deeply against war. But events in Washington would lead him to play a very important role in the war that was coming.

Robert Anderson (1805–1871) fought in the Civil War and the Mexican-American War (1846–1848).

CHAPTER 3

THE SECESSION CRISIS

The presidential election of 1860 tore the country apart. The Republican candidate was Abraham Lincoln. He was not opposed to slavery, but he was against it in new states. Southerners saw this as a personal attack. Several states, including South Carolina, said they would **secede** if Lincoln won.

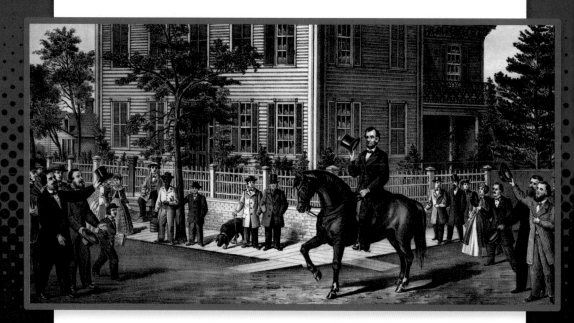

Lincoln ran his campaign from his home in Springfield, Illinois.

No Southern state voted for Lincoln to become president.

On November 6, 1860, Lincoln won the election. The mood in the South, especially Charleston, was tense. On election day, soldiers from Fort Moultrie went to town for supplies. They were threatened by townspeople. They returned to the fort empty-handed.

Fort Moultrie is not just one fort. It is a series of
fortifications and ammunition storage buildings that run
along the edge of the island.

On December 20, the South Carolina General **Assembly** met. The members talked about the election. Most of the assembly members were wealthy white men. Most of them enslaved people. They voted 169–0 to secede. According to the assembly, "A geographical line has been drawn across the Union, and all the States north of that line have united in the election of a man to the high office of President of the United States, whose opinions and purposes are hostile to slavery." They encouraged other states to follow their example. It seemed all paths for the nation were leading to war.

At the fort, Anderson was worried. He knew he didn't have enough men at Fort Moultrie. He made the decision to move his troops to the newer, stronger Fort Sumter. He hoped they could wait out whatever happened. But he also knew the move would anger the South Carolina government. If he was attacked, it would begin a civil war. On the night of December 26, he and his men rowed their way across the harbor to their new home.

CHAPTER 4

THE BATTLE OF FORT SUMTER

Anderson had been right—the people of South Carolina were angry. They believed that the forts were on Confederate land. That made it a Confederate fort. The forts had been on loan to the federal government. Now that the state and the Union were separate, the state wanted Union troops to leave. They did not need to be moving to the most defendable fort.

Fort Sumter has high walls made of heavy stonework.

Anderson's move showed that the Union troops would not give up without a fight. The South Carolina **militia** began assembling. Over the next few months, thousands of soldiers showed up.

On January 9, things turned violent. The *Star of the West*, a merchant vessel, sailed into the harbor. It carried more troops and supplies for Fort Sumter. South Carolina's leaders knew that with more troops, Fort Sumter would be much harder to capture. The militia opened fire. The *Star of the West* was forced to turn back.

The *Star of the West* was a privately owned steamship hired to transport troops and goods for the U.S. military.

Outside South Carolina, the country was falling apart. Alabama, Florida, Georgia, Louisiana, Mississippi, and Texas all seceded. In February, representatives of these states met. They formed a new nation: the Confederate States of America. Former Mississippi senator Jefferson Davis was elected as president.

Davis named Pierre Gustave Toutant Beauregard as the Confederacy's first brigadier general. Beauregard was an artillery expert. He had been a student and good friend of Anderson. He was given orders to report to Charleston. There, he would prepare the Confederate troops. They would capture Fort Sumter.

Beauregard served at other major Civil War battles, including Shiloh and the First Battle of Bull Run.

FRIENDS TO ENEMIES

Before the war, Jefferson Davis had served in the army. He had also been the nation's secretary of war. Davis and Robert Anderson had served together and remained good friends. After the war, Davis was captured and imprisoned for two years. He was pardoned of treason by President Andrew Johnson.

The outlook was not looking good for Anderson and his men. Fort Sumter gave them a good defensive position. However, their food stores were running low. With limited ammunition and few men, they could not hold out for long. On April 4, President Lincoln sent them new supplies. But the Confederates got wind of the plan. Beauregard was ordered to make sure the supplies did not reach Fort Sumter.

Jefferson Davis (1808–1889)

Beauregard sent messengers to Fort Sumter. They asked Anderson to surrender. Anderson refused. He knew supplies were coming. He might have to defend the ships. Beauregard warned Anderson that he would attack in one hour. The first shot of the Civil War was fired on April 12, 1861, at 4:30 a.m.

For two hours, Beauregard's cannons blasted the fort. But the fort was quiet. The Union soldiers did not have enough cloth cartridges to risk wasting shots. Firing into the dark might not do anything. They waited until after breakfast to attack. By this time, the Confederate cannons had already fired more than 200 rounds.

Fort Sumter was the last place of federal power in South Carolina.

Over the next two days, thousands of shots were fired. Luckily, there were no **casualties** on either side during this time. But Fort Sumter was damaged. There was a fatal accident.

The 50,000-pound (22,680-kilogram) Rodman guns at Fort Sumter were the largest cannons in use at the time.

READY, AIM, FIRE!

The cannons used by each side needed at least five soldiers to fire. Two men cleaned and loaded the barrel. Two others were in charge of getting a new cannonball and gunpowder. Finally, a gunner aimed the cannon and fired it. Some cannons needed twice as many men.

The Confederate forces fired heated cannonballs called "hotshot." These caused many fires to start inside the fort. Smoke filled the air. Soldiers had to crawl back and forth between their cannons. At 1:00 p.m. on April 13, the flagpole fell. The Confederates thought this might mean a victory was near. Messengers were sent to the fort. They waved a white flag. The flag let the Union forces know they were peaceful.

Confederate guns around the harbor fired on Fort Sumter.

Major Anderson surrendered at around 2:30 p.m.

The Confederates told Anderson he and his men must give up the fort. Anderson knew they could not hold out any longer. They were out of ammunition and supplies. Anderson surrendered. The booming of cannons across the harbor stopped. The Battle of Fort Sumter was over.

CHAPTER 5

THE COST AND THE PRIZE

The Union troops left the next day. The resupply boats sent by President Lincoln took them to New York. When they arrived, Anderson and his men were treated as heroes.

Confederate forces took over Fort Sumter. In the coming war, it would be a key defense for the harbor.

The Confederacy's attack on Fort Sumter shook the nation. Four more states seceded. President Lincoln called for 75,000 **recruits** to join the Union Army. During the next four years, battles were fought across the nation. The conflict would see around 750,000 soldiers die. But it would also pave the way for the abolition of slavery. America was never the same.

FACT

Union forces finally retook Fort Sumter in February 1865. By that time, the fort was mostly destroyed from heavy artillery fire.

President Lincoln issued the Emancipation Proclamation on January 1, 1863. It committed the Union army to freeing enslaved people in the South.

TIMELINE

NOVEMBER 6, 1860: Abraham Lincoln is elected president of the United States.

NOVEMBER 15, 1860: Major Robert Anderson is ordered to take command of Union forces in Charleston.

DECEMBER 20, 1860: South Carolina secedes from the Union.

DECEMBER 26, 1860: Major Anderson orders his soldiers to transfer to Fort Sumter.

JANUARY 9, 1861: The *Star of the West*, a ship with supplies and reinforcements for Fort Sumter, is attacked in Charleston Harbor and forced to retreat.

FEBRUARY 8, 1861: The Confederate States of America is formed by South Carolina, Mississippi, Florida, Alabama, Georgia, Louisiana, and Texas.

APRIL 11, 1861: Major Anderson refuses P.G.T. Beauregard's offer of surrender.

APRIL 12, 1861: The first shot of the American Civil War is fired against Fort Sumter.

APRIL 13, 1861: Major Anderson agrees to leave Fort Sumter.

FEBRUARY 17, 1865: Union forces retake Fort Sumter.

GLOSSARY

abolitionist (ab-uh-LI-shuhn-ist)—a person who worked to end slavery

artillery (ar-TIL-uh-ree)—cannons and other large guns used during battles

assembly (uh-SEM-blee)—a meeting of lots of people

casualty (KAZH-oo-uhl-tee)—someone who is injured, captured, killed, or missing in an accident, a disaster, or a war

crossfire (KROS-fyre)—gunfire coming from more than one place

garrison (GA-ruh-suhn)—a group of soldiers based in a town and ready to defend it

militia (muh-LISH-uh)—a group of volunteer citizens who serve as soldiers in emergencies

political party (puh-LIT-uh-kuhl PAR-tee)—a group of people who share similar beliefs about how the government should operate

recruit (ri-KROOT)—new member of the armed forces

secede (si-SEED)—to formally withdraw from a group or an organization, often to form another organization

READ MORE

Berglund, Bruce. *Drummer Boys Lead the Charge: Courageous Kids of the Civil War.* North Mankato, MN: Capstone, 2021.

Gunderson, Jessica. *Assassination of Abraham Lincoln: A Day That Changed America.* North Mankato, MN: Capstone, 2022.

Smith, Elliott. *Hidden Heroes in the Civil War.* Minneapolis: Lerner Publications, 2023.

INTERNET SITES

American Battlefield Trust: Fort Sumter
battlefields.org/learn/civil-war/battles/fort-sumter

Britannica Kids: Fort Sumter
kids.britannica.com/kids/article/Fort-Sumter/599831

History for Kids: Battle of Fort Sumter
historyforkids.net/battle-of-fort-sumter.html

INDEX

Author Biography

Isaac Kerry is an author, stay-at-home dad, and firefighter. He lives in Minnesota with his wife, two daughters, and an assortment of four-legged creatures. He can often be found writing, wrangling children, or riding big red trucks. When not engaged in these pursuits, he loves reading, working out, and board games.